anything

Kids Top 10
Pet Fish

Dana Meachen Rau

Enslow Elementary

an imprint of

Enslow Publishers, Inc.

40 Industrial Road
Box 398
Berkeley Heights, NJ 07922
USA

http://www.enslow.com

American Humane Association is the country's first national humane organization and the only one dedicated to protecting both children and animals. Since 1877, American Humane Association has been at the forefront of virtually every major advance in protecting our most vulnerable from cruelty, abuse and neglect. Today we're also leading the way in understanding the human-animal bond and its role in therapy, medicine and society. American Humane Association reaches millions of people every day through groundbreaking research, education, training and services that span a wide network of organizations, agencies and businesses. You can help make a difference, too. Visit American Humane Association at www.americanhumane.org today.

To Our Readers: We have done our best to make sure all Internet addresses in this book were active and appropriate when we went to press. However, the author and the publisher have no control over and assume no liability for the material available on those Internet sites or on other Web sites they may link to. Any comments or suggestions can be sent by e-mail to comments@enslow.com or to the address on the back cover.

Every effort has been made to locate all copyright holders of material used in this book. If any errors or omissions have occurred, corrections will be made in future editions of this book.

♻ Enslow Publishers, Inc., is committed to printing our books on recycled paper. The paper in every book contains 10% to 30% post-consumer waste (PCW). The cover board on the outside of each book contains 100% PCW. Our goal is to do our part to help young people and the environment too!

Enslow Elementary, an imprint of Enslow Publishers, I
Enslow Elementary® is a registered trademark of Enslow Publishers, Inc.

Copyright © 2015 by Enslow Publishers, Inc.

Originally published as *Top 10 Fish for Kids* in 2009.

Library of Congress Cataloging-in-Publication Dat

Rau, Dana Meachen, 1971– author.
  [Top 10 fish for kids]
  Kids top 10 pet fish / Dana Meachen Rau.
    pages cm. — (American Humane Association
      top 10 pets for kids)
  "Originally published as Top 10 fish for kids in 2009."
  Summary: "Discusses the best ten fish for kids to kee
    as pets and includes each species' appearance, gen
    behavior, and special needs"— Provided by publis
  Audience: K to grade 3.
  Includes bibliographical references and index.
    ISBN 978-0-7660-6640-3
  1. Aquarium fishes—Juvenile literature. I. Title.
    II. Title: Kids top ten pet fish.
  SF457.25.R38 2015
  639.34—dc23
                                    2014026872

Future Editions:
Paperback ISBN: 978-0-7660-6641-0
EPUB ISBN: 978-0-7660-6642-7
Single-User PDF ISBN: 978-0-7660-6643-4
Multi-User PDF ISBN: 978-0-7660-6644-1

Printed in the United States of America

102014 Bang Printing, Brainerd, Minn.

10 9 8 7 6 5 4 3 2 1

Interior Photo Credits: iStockphoto.com: Eric Isselée, pp. 25 (betta), 31 (clownfish), 33 (goldfish); gmnicholas, p. 6; Krzysztof Rafa, p. 10; Lise Gagne, p. 7; Rosica Daskalova, p. 22; Sue McDonald, p. 35 (guppy). Shutterstock.com: bluehand, p. 37 (molly); cbpix, p. 30; Christina Richards, p. 15; Dmitry Onishchik, p. 14; Dmitry V. Petrenko, p. 38; Dobermaraner, p. 39 (neon tetra); Eric Isselée, p. 8 (seahorse); foto76, p. 20; Grigorev Mikhail, p. 40; iliuta goean, p. 36; Julia Kuznetsova, p. 17; KAMONRAT, p. 24; Kristof Degreef, p. 44; Levent Konuk, p. 16 (clownfish); Mark Aplet, p. 26; Mirek Kijewski, p. 32; mnoor, p. 34; Nantawat Chotsuwan, p. 42 (guppy); Napat, p. 47; Paul Prescott, p. 13; Pavel Vakhrushev, p. 1 (fish); Pixel Memoirs, p. 23 (angelfish); S-F, pp. 4, 9, 19; Topimages, p. 41 (platy); Vangert, p. 5 (goldfish). © Thinkstock: garth11/iStock, p. 43; IMNATURE/iStock, p. 28; Michael Stubblefield/iStock, p. 27 (chromis); Nut1983/iStock, p. 21.

Cover Credit: Andrey Armyagov/Shutterstock.com (goldfish).

The top ten fish are approved by the American Humane Association and are listed alphabetically.

Contents

A home aquarium is a fascinating underwater world. You create it yourself, and fill it with your own fish.

So You Want to Get a Fish?

The underwater world is a fascinating place. There are fish of all shapes, sizes, and colors. You can learn to scuba dive to get a look at these interesting swimmers up close. Or you can watch them right in your home!

Kids Top 10 Pet Fish

A person who keeps an aquarium is called an aquarist.

If you are thinking of getting a pet fish, make sure it is a family decision. Talk together about what kind of pet you would like. Fish are a lot of fun to watch. But that is about all you can do with them. You cannot cuddle or play with a fish like you can with a cat or a dog.

As with any pet, you are responsible for taking care of a fish. You have to make sure it has a good home (tank), gets the right food to eat, and stays healthy.

So You Want to Get a Fish?

Do you have time every day to feed your fish? Do you have time every week to clean the tank? Will you be willing to take care of a fish for its whole life? While fish can get sick easily and may only live a few weeks or months, many live for a few years. Others, with the right care, can live even longer. Keeping a home aquarium is a lot of work.

Fish also need a lot of equipment. After you decide what kind of fish you want, you will need to get and set up the equipment. Your first stop will be the pet store or aquarium store.

Parts of a Fish

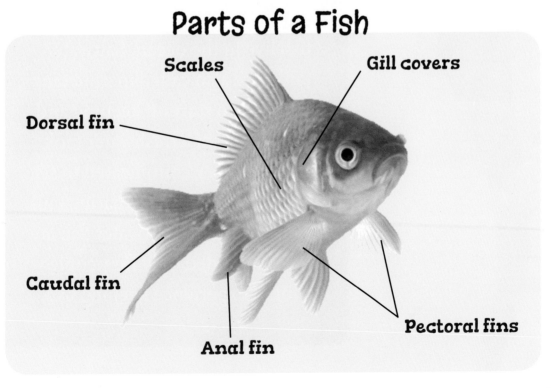

Scales

Gill covers

Dorsal fin

Caudal fin

Anal fin

Pectoral fins

An Aquarium to Call Home

There are two types of fish— freshwater and saltwater. In the wild, freshwater fish live in lakes, ponds, and streams. Saltwater fish live in the ocean. Saltwater tanks are also called marine tanks. It is best to start off keeping and taking care of a freshwater tank. It can be very complicated to set up and take care of a marine tank. Because of this, saltwater fish are recommended only for people with a lot of experience keeping fish.

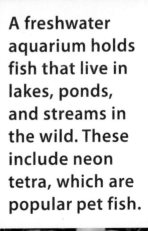

A freshwater aquarium holds fish that live in lakes, ponds, and streams in the wild. These include neon tetra, which are popular pet fish.

Tanks and Supplies

Some experts say that you should start with a twenty-five- to fifty-gallon tank. Others say a ten-gallon tank is fine. The biggest tank you can afford (and that you have room for) will be the best choice. It will give your fish more room to swim and less of a chance of getting sick from dirty water.

Live plants make great hiding places for fish in an aquarium. They also help keep the water clean. Like your fish, they need special care.

An Aquarium to Call Home

Your tank will also need a hood with a light. Light will help your fish stay healthy. If you have live plants in your tank, they need light to survive. You will need a heater and a thermometer to check the water temperature. Finally, the tank needs a filter. The filter sucks in water, cleans it, then puts it back into the tank.

You will need gravel and decorations. You can use live plants in the tanks, too. Live plants help keep the water healthy. But they need special care. Ask at the pet store to find out the best type of plant for the fish you are planning to take home. You can also decorate the tank with plastic plants made especially for home aquariums. Other aquarium decorations, such as a treasure chest or castle, are fun. These decorations, made especially for fish tanks, give your fish places to hide.

Setting Up the Tank

Now that you have all the equipment, it is time to start setting up. First, make sure you choose a strong and solid stand or piece of furniture to hold your tank. Your tank can weigh a hundred pounds or more when filled with water.

Where should you place the tank? First of all, it will need to be near an electrical outlet to plug in the filter, light, and heater. It should also be near a water source because you will need to change the water regularly. Remember, water and electricity can be dangerous together. So you need to find a place where your tank cannot be knocked over. You should not put it in an area where there is a lot of activity. A corner is often a good place.

Fish do not like changes in water temperature. Do not put the tank near windows where the sun can heat up their water. Also avoid any area near a heating vent, fireplace, or radiator. Instead, try to choose an area for the tank where the water temperature is likely to remain the same all the time.

Fish are also very sensitive to sound. So do not put the tank right near a television or stereo where they might feel a lot of vibration. For the same reason, never bang on the glass to get your fish's attention.

To fill the tank, use water from the faucet that has been tested and adjusted to make sure it is just right for your fish to survive. It may have some things in it that

An Aquarium to Call Home

Be sure to put your fish tank on a sturdy piece of furniture. The tank might weigh a hundred pounds or more when it is filled with water.

An aquarium thermometer is important for making sure the water temperature always stays the same.

can harm your fish, such as a chemical called chlorine. You should also test the water with something called a pH kit. With this test you can make sure the water is safe for your fish.

Talk to someone at the store where you bought your fish for more information and details about setting up your tank. He or she will know a lot about fish tanks and can probably give you good advice.

It is important to use a pH kit to test the water in your tank. This will tell you that the water is safe for your fish.

9.0

8.5

8.0

7.5

aissez le
ce qu'il n'y

äbchen bis zur
lassen.

Choosing Your Pet Fish

There are so many different types of fish, it can be difficult to decide which kind is right for you. And how many should you get?

There are a lot of things to think about when trying to decide which of the many types of fish to get.

Kids Top 10 Pet Fish

The number of fish that can live in your tank depends on the size of the tank. A general rule is one inch of fish per gallon of water, as long as the fish are slim and no more than three or four inches long. For example, a twenty-five-gallon tank can be a comfortable home for twenty-five "inches" of fish. In other words, if your fish are all about two inches long, that means about twelve fish.

It is a good idea to start with just three or four fish. Make sure to pick a kind of fish that can survive in the harsh water conditions of a new tank. These fish will "prepare" the tank for more fish.

When fish "breathe" through their gills, and when they go to the bathroom, their waste contains ammonia. Too much ammonia in the water can kill fish. But luckily, there are types of bacteria that need ammonia to live. They change the ammonia to a less harmful substance so the water is safe for the fish.

This process takes a few weeks. Then you can have the water tested to be sure that there are enough bacteria now to handle the waste of more fish.

When you go to pick out your fish, you will notice that some aquarium fish are very expensive, while others cost less. But price is not the only thing to think about.

For a community tank, it is very important to choose fish that can live together peacefully.

If you want to have a community tank, where there will be more than one fish, you have to find fish that will get along with each other. Some fish are very aggressive. They might eat all of the food so that more timid fish cannot get to their meal. Some fish eat smaller fish. Some like to be in a school, or group of fish. Some fish lay eggs. Some fish are livebearers, which means they give birth to live young. A male and female fish of the same kind may mate and give you many more baby fish.

Kids Top 10 Pet Fish

Look for a healthy fish. Check that it has clear eyes and that it does not have any spots or sores on its body. It should be active and alert. If any fish in the tank looks sick, buy from a different tank. Diseases spread easily in water.

Each type of fish has its own needs. Some prefer to live in a tank by themselves.

Fish need several minutes to get used to the temperature of the water in a new tank.

Once you have chosen your fish and brought it home, float the bag on the top of the tank for about fifteen minutes. This will help the fish get used to the temperature of the water. Then add some water from the tank to the fish's bag a few times to help it get used to the new water. After about half an hour, move your fish from the bag into the tank with a soft net.

Angelfish are originally from the central Amazon River in South America.

Appearance

- Come in many colors, such as silver, black, and gold
- Very long fins
- Flat, triangle-shaped body
- Grow to about 5 inches in length

Angelfish like to hide. Plenty of aquarium plants will give them great hiding places.

Chapter 1

Angelfish

When a female and male angelfish get together, they stay together for life. They mate only with each other. In the wild, angelfish live in the central Amazon River in South America.

Special Needs

Angelfish need a warm freshwater tank with water temperature between 72° and 82° F. They need a deep tank because of their body shape, as well as places to hide. They will be healthiest if you feed them a mixture of flake, frozen, and live food.

General Behavior

Angelfish:

1. are peaceful fish and can be good in a community tank if they were raised in it. Sometimes older angelfish and those that are mating can be aggressive.

2. may get bothered by fish that like to nip long fins.

3. might eat smaller fish, such as neon tetras.

Bettas are sometimes called Siamese fighting fish.

Like other fish, bettas have gills. But they also have a special organ that lets them breathe air from the water's surface.

Appearance

- Come in many colors, such as red, blue, green, black, and yellow
- Long, flowing fins. Females have shorter fins than males.
- Grow to about 2.5 inches in length

Chapter 2

Betta (Siamese Fighting Fish)

Bettas are sometimes called Siamese fighting fish. They are originally from Thailand (once called Siam) and other areas of Southern Asia.

Special Needs

Bettas need a freshwater tank with the water at a temperature between 75° and 86° F. They may jump out of the water, so you must cover the tank. Use something that still lets air through, such as a screen.

General Behavior

Bettas:

1. are peaceful unless two males are put in a tank together. Males will fight each other until one dies. Some tanks have special barriers, or boxes that hang off the side to keep males separate.

2. should not be kept in community tanks because they will eat smaller fish and may get bothered by fish that like to nip long fins.

3. do best by themselves.

Blue-green chromis get along with most other fish.

Blue-green chromis are saltwater fish that swim in a school, or group.

Appearance

- Greenish coloring over the whole body
- Short, pointed fins and a forked tail fin
- Grow to about 2 inches in length

Chapter 3

Blue-Green Chromis

Blue-green chromis are a type of damselfish. Most damselfish are aggressive and like to be alone. Blue-green chromis, however, swim in schools and get along with other fish. They are from coral reefs in the Indian Ocean and western Pacific. They are saltwater fish. You may need the help of an adult to care for them properly.

General Behavior

Blue-green chromis:

1. are peaceful and shy.
2. are good for community tanks because they get along with most other fish.
3. like to swim in a school, so get at least four of them for your tank.

Special Needs

Blue-green chromis need a marine (saltwater) tank with water temperature between 75° and 82° F. Be on the lookout for blue-green chromis that spend their time hiding. They may feel threatened by other fish in the tank. Having a small school of blue-green chromis can prevent that, since they feel safer in a group.

Brazilian sea horses spend time holding onto grass with their curly tails.

Appearance

- Come in black, brown, and yellow. Some have bands and spots of color.
- Curly tail, horse-shaped head, and long snout
- Grow to about 4 to 8 inches in length

Brazilian sea horses swim slowly. They should not share a tank with faster fish that will eat up all the food.

Chapter 4

Brazilian Sea Horse

Brazilian sea horses swim vertically (up and down), not horizontally (side-to-side) like other fish. They are originally from the western Caribbean. Many colorful examples were found in the waters off Brazil, which is how they got their name. They are saltwater fish. You may need the help of an adult to care for them properly.

General Behavior

Brazilian sea horses:

1. are peaceful fish.
2. swim slowly.
3. live best as a male and female pair or with other Brazilian sea horses.
4. spend time holding onto grass with their curly tails.
5. are carnivores (meat eaters), so they like to eat live and frozen saltwater shrimp.

Special Needs

Brazilian sea horses need a marine tank with water temperature between 72° and 82° F. The tank should be at least twenty-nine to fifty-five gallons. It should have lots of plants that the fish can grasp with their tails. Brazilian sea horses cannot be in a tank with fast-moving water because they are not strong swimmers.

Clownfish are saltwater fish.

The waving tentacles of an anemone are home to these two clownfish in the wild.

Appearance

- Yellow-orange body with three bands of white that have thin black bands
- Double fins
- Grow to about 2.75 inches in length

Chapter 5

Clownfish

Clownfish are also called anemone (a-NEM-a-nee) fish. This is because in the wild they live among the tentacles (arms) of anemone. Anemone are sea animals related to corals and jellyfish.

Clownfish are originally from the coral reefs of the Indian Ocean and western Pacific. They are saltwater fish. You may need the help of an adult to care for them properly.

General Behavior

Clownfish:

1. are peaceful fish. However, a male clownfish will chase fish away from its territory, especially other male clownfish.

2. live best alone or as a male and female pair.

3. are aggressive eaters.

Special Needs

Clownfish need a marine tank with water temperature between 75° and 82° F. They are used to living among anemone in the wild, so their tank will need anemone or a cave-like place for the clownfish to hide.

Goldfish were one of the first fish to be kept and bred as pets.

Goldfish will eat as much food as you give them, so be careful not to overfeed them.

Appearance

- Red-orange in color
- Rounded fins, forked caudal fins
- Can grow from 2 inches to 2 feet in length, depending on their tank environment

Chapter 6

Goldfish

Goldfish are a favorite first fish for many people because they are so easy to take care of. Goldfish are originally from Asia and parts of Eastern Europe. They were one of the first fish to be kept and bred as pets.

General Behavior

Goldfish:

1. are peaceful fish.

2. are good for community tanks with other fish that prefer cold water, but live best with other goldfish.

Special Needs

Goldfish need a cold, freshwater tank with water temperature between 64º to 70º F, so they do not do well with tropical freshwater fish that need warmer water. Goldfish grow fast and create a lot of waste, so be sure the tank is big enough. Never put them in a fishbowl, which does not have enough room for the fish to swim, and will not let them get enough oxygen. Goldfish need a good filter that cleans the water and puts in a lot of air. They also need places to hide.

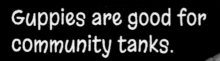

Guppies are good for community tanks.

Appearance

- Come in red, green, black, and many other colors and combinations

- Males are colorful, while females are a dull gray.

- Long, flowing fins in different shapes, such as rounded, swordtail, and fantail. Females have much smaller fins than males.

- Grow to about 1.25 inches in length

Guppies give birth to live fry. Plants make a good hiding place for the fry so they are not eaten by other fish.

Chapter 7

Guppy

Have you ever heard anyone described as a "small fry"? "Fry" is the term for baby fish. You will soon have your own crowd of small fry if you decide to put male and female guppies in your tank! In the wild, these fish live in the waters of the Caribbean Islands, upper South America, and Central America.

General Behavior

Guppies:

1. are peaceful fish.
2. are good fish to have in community tanks.
3. may get bothered by fish that nip at long fins. They also nip at the long fins of other fish.
4. could be eaten if put in a tank with larger fish.
5. mate easily.

Special Needs

Guppies need a freshwater tank with water temperature between 72° and 82° F. Guppies like their water a little salty, so you can add about one teaspoon of aquarium salt per gallon of water (be sure never to use regular table salt!).

Mollies have a variety of fin shapes. This is a sailfin molly.

Appearance

- Can be green, black, silver, or gold
- A variety of fin types, such as sailfin and lyre tail. The common molly, also known as the short finned molly, has small fins.

Mollies are live-bearing fish, which means they give birth to live young.

Chapter 8

Molly

In a group of mollies, one fish usually becomes dominant over the others. This is one reason that mollies are fun to watch. These fish are originally from the southern United States, South America, and Central America.

General Behavior

Mollies:

1. do very well in community tanks.

2. may nip at slower fish.

Special Needs

Mollies need a freshwater tank with water temperature between 72° and 82° F. They especially like plenty of plants for hiding. Mollies also like their water to be a little salty, so you can add about one teaspoon of aquarium salt per gallon of water.

Neon tetras like to swim in a school.

Tiny neon tetras make a colorful display as they swim around in a school.

Appearance

- Slim bodies with a blue stripe from head to tail, silver on top, and red on the bottom

- Very pointed fins and a forked caudal fin

- Grow to about 1 inch in length

Chapter 9

Neon Tetra

A neon tetra's colors are brightest when it is active during the day. The colors are duller when the fish is resting at night. Neon tetras are originally from the rivers of South America.

Special Needs

Neon tetras need a warm freshwater tank with water temperature between 72° and 82° F. They need lots of space to swim, since they are a schooling fish. But they also like lots of hiding places. Neon tetras cannot be in a tank with large fish because they will be eaten. They are best with fish of their own size.

General Behavior

Neon tetras:

1. are shy.

2. are good fish to have in community tanks.

3. like to swim in a school, so you should get five or more.

Platys are active and need room to swim around.

Platys like a well-lit tank with plants to hide in and plenty of room to swim around.

Appearance

- Come in many colors, such as red, blue, black, gold, and even rainbow. Females can be a little duller.

- Rounded caudal fin and a large dorsal fin

- Grow to about 1.5 inches in length

Chapter 10

Platy

Platys are sometimes called moonfish because of a crescent shape at the base of their tails, especially in gold ones. These fish are originally from the Atlantic coastal waters of Mexico, Guatemala, and Honduras in Central America.

General Behavior

Platys:

1. are peaceful fish.
2. are good fish to have in community tanks.
3. can be active and might bother slower moving fish, such as angelfish.
4. mate easily, so a male and female in the same tank will make many fry.

Special Needs

Platys need a freshwater tank with water temperature between 72º and 82º F. They like their water to be a little salty, so you can add about one teaspoon of aquarium salt per gallon of water.

Keeping Your Fish Healthy

One of the most important things you will need to do to keep your fish healthy is to change the water in the tank every one to two weeks to keep it clean. When you add new water, be sure it is treated to adjust its pH or chlorine level. Also make sure it is about the same temperature as the water in the tank. Every four to six weeks, you will also need to clean or change the filter.

Keeping Your Fish Healthy

Feeding

You will need to feed your fish twice a day, morning and night. Be very careful not to overfeed them. You should feed your fish only as much as they can eat in three to five minutes. The type of food will depend on your fish.

Health Care

After many weeks of watching your fish, you will know how each one behaves. You will be able to tell when any of your fish are sick because it will look or act different than usual.

It is important to make sure that the filter in your tank is working correctly so the water stays clean and your fish stay healthy.

Notice the way your fish swims. Is it darting around the tank, or is it moving slowly? Is it at the surface, or is it lying on the bottom of the tank? Look at your fish's body.

Watch your fish every day and get to know their normal behavior. This will help you recognize if one of them becomes ill.

Keeping Your Fish Healthy

Are its eyes cloudy or fins split? Has it changed color or developed spots? This might mean your fish is sick.

Most illnesses are caused by the water in the tank. You must regularly check the water with a test kit. And be sure to check that the filter is working correctly. If needed, clean the tank and bring in some new, clean water.

It is also important to vacuum the gravel in your tank every so often. Uneaten food can settle in the gravel and decay, making the water dirty.

If a fish dies, remove it from the tank with a net as soon as possible so it will not make the other fish sick.

Do not flush a dead fish down the toilet. It will get into waterways and might spread its illness to other fish in the wild. You can bury your fish outdoors in the ground. Or you can place it in a bag and put it in the trash.

Unlike other pets, fish do not need to be petted, brushed, or taken on walks. They do not need toys to play with or constant attention from you. But they do rely on you to survive. It is your job as their owner to make their tank a place where they can live a happy and healthy life.

Glossary

anemone—An animal with long arm-like tentacles that gives clownfish a place to hide.

chlorine—A chemical in water that can be dangerous to fish.

community tank—A tank with many types of fish living together.

filter—A part of a tank that sucks in water, cleans it, then puts it back into the tank.

fry—Baby fish.

gills—Parts of a fish's body that allow it to breathe under water.

live-bearer—A fish that gives birth to live young instead of laying eggs.

marine tank—A saltwater tank.

pH kit—A kit that tests the water in a fish tank. It will tell you if the water is safe for fish.

school—A group of fish of the same kind.

territory—An area an animal lives in that it tries to protect.

Further Reading

Lundblad, Kristina, and Bobbie Kalman. *Animals Called Fish.* New York: Crabtree Publishing Company, 2005.

MacAulay, Kelley, and Bobbie Kalman. *Goldfish.* New York: Crabtree Publishing Company, 2005.

Richardson, Adele. *Caring For Your Fish.* Mankato, Minn.: Capstone Press, 2007.

Silverstein, Virginia, Alvin Silverstein, and Laura Silverstein Nunn. *Fabulous Fish.* Brookfield, Conn.: Twenty-First Century Books, 2003.

Index

A

anemone, 31
angelfish, 22–23, 41
aquariums (tanks), 6, 7, 8–14, 18, 20, 21, 23, 25, 27, 29, 31, 33, 35, 37, 39, 41, 42, 43, 45

B

bettas (Siamese fighting fish), 24–25
blue-green chromis, 26–27
Brazilian sea horses, 28–29

C

clownfish, 30–31
community tanks, 19, 23, 25, 27, 33, 35, 37, 39, 41

F

feeding, 6–7, 23, 43
freshwater fish, 8, 22–23, 24–25, 32–33, 34–35, 36–37, 38–39, 40–41
freshwater tanks, 8, 23, 25, 33, 35, 37, 39, 41
fry, 35, 41

G

goldfish, 32–33
guppies, 34–35

H

health, 6, 10–11, 20, 23, 42–45

M

marine tanks, 8, 27, 29, 31
mollies, 36–37

N

neon tetras, 23, 38–39

P

plants, 11, 29, 37
platys, 40–41

R

responsibility, 6–7, 45

S

saltwater fish, 8, 26–27, 28–29, 30–31
schooling, 19, 27, 39

W

water, 10, 11, 12, 14, 18, 20, 21, 29, 33, 35, 37, 41, 42, 45